Living For God The Call To Be A Living Sacrifice

Joshua Rhoades

Published by Joshua Paul Rhoades, 2024.

While every precaution has been taken in the preparation of this book, the publisher assumes no responsibility for errors or omissions, or for damages resulting from the use of the information contained herein.

LIVING FOR GOD THE CALL TO BE A LIVING SACRIFICE

First edition. September 24, 2024.

Copyright © 2024 Joshua Rhoades.

ISBN: 979-8227560308

Written by Joshua Rhoades.

Also by Joshua Rhoades

Courage Under Fire: David's Stand On The Battlefield
Jonah's Journey: Voices Of Redemption And Lessons In Obedience
The Furnace Of Faith: 12 Principles From The Heat Of Faith
Whispers of Hope: Inspiring Stories of Men's Prayers In Scripture
Frontier Legends: The Oregon Dream
Elijah: A Beacon Of Boldness
HOOK, LINE & SAVIOUR - Faith Reflections from Fishing
Driven By Faith: Motor Racing Inspired Christian Life
30 Day Devotional - Bold and Strong- Coffee Devotions for a
Courageous Christian Walk
Authentic Christianity: The Heart of Old Time Religion
Consider The Ant - God's Tiny Preachers
Flee Fornication: The Plea For Purity
Renewed Hope- How to Find Encouragement in God
Sounding The Call - The Voice of Conviction
The Altar - Where Heaven Meets Earth
The Bible's Battlefields- Timeless Lessons from Ancient Wars
The Sacred Art of Silence - How Silence Speaks in Scripture
Under Fire- The Sanctity of the Traditional Biblical Home
Who Is on the Lord's Side? A Call to Righteousness
What Is Truth? - From Skepticism to Submission
First and Goal- Faith and Football Fundamentals
From Dugout to Devotion- Spiritual Lessons from Baseball
Par for the Course- Faith and Fairways
The Believer's Pace- Tools for Running Life's Marathon

Dedication

To you, dear reader, I dedicate this book with a heart full of prayer and hope. You are embarking on a journey that is not for the faint of heart. The call to live for God as a living sacrifice, as taught in Romans 12:1-2, is one of the most profound challenges we will ever face. It requires the surrender of everything we hold dear, laying down our own will and desires, and trusting fully in the One who gave His life for us. Yet, it is also the greatest privilege and honor to live for God, to be set apart for His purpose, and to be transformed by the renewing of our minds.

As you read these pages, I know you will be challenged. You may find moments where your heart resists the idea of surrender, where the cost seems too great, and the path too difficult. But I want you to know that God is with you every step of the way. He sees your struggles, He understands your fears, and He knows your weaknesses. Yet, He calls you still. He calls you to something greater than comfort or ease—He calls you to a life of meaning, a life that reflects His glory and advances His kingdom.

To be a living sacrifice is not a call to lose yourself but to find your true identity in Christ. It is a call to live beyond the limitations of this world, to experience the fullness of life in God's presence, and to become a vessel of His love, peace, and truth in a world that desperately needs it. This path is not without pain, but it is paved with eternal reward. As you surrender, God will mold and shape you into the image of His Son, Jesus Christ, and through that transformation, you will discover the true purpose for which you were created.

I want to remind you that this journey is not meant to be walked alone. As you sacrifice your own desires for God's will, as you seek to renew your mind and resist the pressures of this world, remember that you are part of a family—a body of believers who are walking the same road. Together, we are called to encourage, uplift, and support one another in our pursuit of holiness.

I pray that as you read this book, you will feel God's presence beside you, urging you forward when you feel like turning back, whispering His love into your heart when you feel weary, and reminding you that your life, offered to Him as a living sacrifice, is a beautiful and powerful act of worship. You are seen. You are loved. And your sacrifice is precious in His sight.

May this journey be one that transforms you, challenges you, and draws you closer to the heart of God. You are not just a reader—you are a living, breathing sacrifice, set apart for the glory of your Creator. This book is for you, with the hope that through its pages, you will come to know the deep, abiding joy that comes from living entirely for Him.

With all my heart, I dedicate this to you, the one who is willing to answer the call. May God bless you richly as you live for Him.

Introduction

"Living for God: The Call to Be a Living Sacrifice" is a profound exploration of what it truly means to dedicate every aspect of our lives to God, inspired by the powerful message in Romans 12:1-2. This book peers into the heart of Christian discipleship, where the call to present ourselves as living sacrifices goes beyond mere religious duties or outward displays of faith. It challenges readers to embrace a life of total surrender, where every thought, action, and desire is aligned with God's will. The concept of being a living sacrifice is not just about making sacrifices for the sake of obedience; it is about a complete transformation that begins in the mind and overflows into every part of our existence. In a world that constantly pressures us to conform to its standards, this book provides a roadmap for resisting those influences and instead embracing the transformative power of God's Word. Through thoughtful reflections, practical applications, and deep spiritual insights, "Living for God" invites readers to experience the joy, peace, and fulfillment that come from living in total alignment with God's purpose. It is a call to step out of the shallow waters of superficial faith and dive into the depths of a life fully devoted to God—a life that not only reflects His love and truth but also shines as a beacon of hope in a world that desperately needs it. Whether you are a new believer seeking to understand what it means to follow Christ or a seasoned Christian looking to deepen your walk with God, this book offers the encouragement and guidance needed to live out the radical, transformative call of being a living sacrifice in today's world.

Chapter 1 – The Dedication

Romans 12:1-2 is a powerful and important passage in the Bible that talks about how we should live our lives as Christians. These verses teach us about the concept of dedication, especially in the context of presenting our bodies as a living sacrifice to God. The idea of dedication is central to these verses, as it emphasizes the importance of committing every part of our being to God's service. When we talk about dedication in this sense, we are not just referring to a one-time decision or a simple act of devotion; we are talking about a continuous and wholehearted commitment to God. This means that every aspect of our lives—our thoughts, our actions, our words, and even our bodies—should be dedicated to serving God and following His will.

Presenting our bodies as a living sacrifice is a significant and profound act of dedication because it requires us to surrender our own desires and ambitions to God's greater purpose. In the Old Testament, sacrifices were offered on an altar, where animals were killed and their bodies were given to God as a symbol of atonement for sin. However, in Romans 12:1-2, Paul is urging us to offer ourselves as living sacrifices, which means that instead of offering a dead animal, we are to offer our own lives—alive, breathing, and active—as a sacrifice to God. This living sacrifice is not a one-time event but an ongoing process that involves daily choices and actions that reflect our commitment to God. It requires us to live in a way that is holy and pleasing to God, which is described in the verse as our "reasonable service" or spiritual worship.

Dedication in this context also means being willing to set ourselves apart from the world. Romans 12:2 specifically instructs us not to be conformed to this world, but to be transformed by the renewing of our minds. This transformation is a key aspect of our dedication to God because it involves a complete change in how we think, act, and live. Instead of following the patterns and behaviors of the world, which are often focused on self-interest, materialism, and temporary pleasures, we are called to live in a way that reflects God's values and priorities. This means that our dedication to God should be evident in every area of our lives, including how we treat others, how we spend our time, and how we make decisions.

The process of renewing our minds is crucial for this transformation to take place. It involves immersing ourselves in God's Word, seeking His guidance through prayer, and being open to the work of the Holy Spirit in our lives. As our minds are renewed, we begin to see things from God's perspective, and our desires and priorities begin to align with His will. This renewal is not just about acquiring knowledge or understanding doctrine; it is about allowing God's truth to penetrate our hearts and change us from the inside out. When our minds are renewed, we are better equipped to discern what is the good, acceptable, and perfect will of God, as mentioned in Romans 12:2.

Another important aspect of dedication in Romans 12:1-2 is the idea of total surrender. To present our bodies as a living sacrifice means that we are willing to give up our own will and submit to God's authority in every area of our lives. This can be challenging because it requires us to let go of our own plans and desires and trust that God's plan for us is better. Total surrender involves a deep level of trust in God's goodness and His love for us. It means believing that His ways are higher than our ways and that He knows what is best for us, even when we don't understand it.

Dedication also involves perseverance and endurance. Living as a living sacrifice is not always easy, and there will be times when we are tempted to give up or to conform to the ways of the world. However, true dedication means that we continue to press on, even when it's difficult, trusting that God will give us the strength we need to remain faithful to Him. It means that we are committed to following God, not just when it's convenient or when we feel like it, but in every situation and circumstance.

Moreover, dedication to God as described in Romans 12:1-2 is not just an individual pursuit; it has a communal aspect as well. As believers, we are part of the body of Christ, and our dedication to God should also be reflected in our relationships with others. This means that we should be dedicated to serving and loving others, just as Christ has served and loved us. Our commitment to God should lead us to live in harmony with others, to be generous and compassionate, and to seek the well-being of those around us.

In conclusion, Romans 12:1-2 calls us to a life of dedication to God. This dedication involves presenting our bodies as a living sacrifice, which requires total surrender, perseverance, and a willingness to be set apart from the world. It also involves the renewal of our minds, which enables us to discern God's will and live in a way that is pleasing to Him. Ultimately, our dedication to God should be evident in every aspect of our lives, including our relationships with others, and should reflect a deep and abiding commitment to following Him. As we strive to live out this dedication, we can trust that God will be with us, guiding us and giving us the strength we need to remain faithful to Him.

Chapter 2 – The Devotion

Romans 12:1-2 is a passage that speaks deeply about how we should live our lives as Christians, focusing particularly on the concept of devotion. Devotion, in this context, goes beyond just performing religious duties or following rituals; it means having a heart that is fully aligned with God's will. When we talk about true worship, it is not just about going to church, singing hymns, or praying out loud; it is about giving our entire selves—our thoughts, emotions, actions, and desires—to God in a way that reflects our deep love and commitment to Him. This kind of devotion is about being sincere in our faith and making sure that our worship is not just a show for others to see, but a genuine expression of our relationship with God. In Romans 12:1, Paul urges believers to present their bodies as a living sacrifice, holy and acceptable to God, which he calls our "reasonable service" or spiritual worship. This means that true worship involves offering every part of our lives to God, not just the parts that are convenient or easy. Devotion in this sense requires a whole-hearted commitment to living in a way that pleases God and reflects His character. It means that our actions should flow from a heart that is devoted to God, and our lives should be a testament to His love and grace.

Living with true devotion to God means that we are constantly seeking to align our hearts and minds with His will. This is not always easy because it requires us to let go of our own desires and plans, and instead, seek what God wants for us. It involves trusting that God's ways are higher than our ways and that He knows what is best for us, even when we do not understand it. This level of devotion is about more than just doing good deeds; it is about having a heart that is fully surrendered to God and desires to please Him in everything. In Romans 12:2, Paul goes on to say that we should not be conformed to this world, but be transformed by the renewing of our minds so that we may prove what is that good, acceptable, and perfect will of God. This transformation is a key aspect of true devotion because it involves a change in how we think, act, and live. Instead of following the patterns and behaviors of the world, which are often focused on self-interest and temporary pleasures, we are called to live in a way that reflects God's values and priorities. This means that our devotion to God should be evident in every area of our lives, including how we treat others, how we spend our time, and how we make decisions.

True devotion also means that our worship is not just an outward act, but something that comes from the heart. It is possible to go through the motions of worship without truly being devoted to God. For example, someone might attend church regularly, participate in religious activities, and even pray, but if their heart is not in it, then their worship is not genuine. True devotion means that our worship is sincere and comes from a deep love for God. It means that we are not just going through the motions to impress others or to fulfill a religious obligation, but that we are truly seeking to connect with God and to honor Him with our lives. This kind of devotion requires honesty with ourselves and with God. It means acknowledging when we are struggling or when our hearts are not fully aligned with God's will, and then seeking His help to realign our hearts and minds.

Another important aspect of true devotion is consistency. It is easy to be devoted to God when things are going well, but true devotion means remaining faithful even when times are tough. This means that our commitment to God should not waver based on our circumstances. Whether we are facing challenges or experiencing blessings, our devotion to God should remain constant. This kind of unwavering devotion is a testament to our trust in God and our belief that He is in control of all things. True devotion also involves perseverance. Living a life that is fully devoted to God is not always easy, and there will be times when we are tempted to give up or to conform to the ways of the world. However, true devotion means that we continue to press on, even when it is difficult, trusting that God will give us the strength we need to remain faithful to Him.

Moreover, true devotion to God is not just about our individual relationship with Him, but it also impacts our relationships with others. As believers, we are called to love and serve others, just as Christ has loved and served us. Our devotion to God should lead us to live in harmony with others, to be generous and compassionate, and to seek the well-being of those around us. This means that our devotion to God should be reflected in how we treat others, in our willingness to forgive, and in our desire to build others up rather than tear them down. True devotion means that we are not just focused on our own spiritual growth, but that we are also committed to helping others grow in their relationship with God.

In conclusion, Romans 12:1-2 calls us to a life of true devotion to God. This devotion involves offering every part of our lives to God as a living sacrifice, seeking to align our hearts and minds with His will, and living in a way that reflects His love and grace. True devotion is not just about performing religious duties or following rituals; it is about having a heart that is fully surrendered to God and desires to please Him in everything. It requires consistency, perseverance, and a genuine commitment to living in a way that honors God. As we strive to live out this devotion, we can trust that God will be with us, guiding us and giving us the strength we need to remain faithful to Him. Our true devotion to God should be evident in every aspect of our lives, including our relationships with others, and should reflect a deep and abiding commitment to following Him. As we continue to grow in our devotion to God, we will find that our worship becomes more than just an outward act; it becomes a true expression of our love for God and our desire to live according to His will.

Chapter 3 – The Discernment

Romans 12:1-2 is a passage that offers deep insights into how we should live as Christians, especially focusing on the idea of discernment. Discernment is the ability to judge well and make decisions that align with God's will, and it's crucial for living a life that pleases Him. The passage begins with an appeal for believers to present their bodies as a living sacrifice, holy and acceptable to God, which is described as our "reasonable service" or spiritual worship. This call to offer ourselves to God is about dedicating our entire being—our thoughts, actions, and desires—to Him. But to do this effectively, we need discernment, and that's where the second verse of Romans 12 comes in. It tells us not to be conformed to this world, but to be transformed by the renewing of our minds. This transformation is essential because it helps us to see things from God's perspective, rather than just going along with what the world thinks or values. By renewing our minds, we begin to understand what is truly important, and we gain the ability to discern what is the good, acceptable, and perfect will of God.

Discernment is like a spiritual compass that helps us navigate through life's decisions, big and small, by pointing us toward what God wants for us. Without it, we might find ourselves making choices based on what seems right to us in the moment or what the world around us encourages, but these choices might not align with God's plans for our lives. The world often promotes values that are contrary to what God desires—such as selfishness, materialism, or seeking pleasure above all else. If we conform to these patterns, we risk drifting away from God's will. But when we allow God to renew our minds, we begin to see through the lies of the world and recognize the truth that God reveals in His Word. This truth helps us discern between what is merely good by worldly standards and what is truly good according to God's perfect standard.

Renewing our minds involves immersing ourselves in God's Word, praying, and seeking His guidance in everything we do. As we do this, our thoughts and attitudes start to change. We begin to think less about what we want and more about what God wants. Our priorities shift from pursuing our own desires to seeking first the Kingdom of God and His righteousness. This shift in mindset is crucial because it is only when our minds are aligned with God's truth that we can accurately discern His will. Discernment isn't just about knowing right from wrong; it's about understanding the nuances of God's will in different situations. It's about being able to recognize not just what is acceptable, but what is perfect in God's eyes.

The process of renewing our minds is ongoing. It's not something that happens overnight, but rather something that requires consistent effort and a willingness to grow. We live in a world that constantly bombards us with messages that are contrary to God's Word, so we need to be vigilant in guarding our minds and hearts against these influences. This might mean being selective about what we watch, listen to, or read, and making sure that we're spending time in God's Word daily. The more we fill our minds with God's truth, the easier it becomes to discern His will. It's like training our minds to recognize what is true, noble, right, pure, lovely, admirable, excellent, or praiseworthy, as Philippians 4:8 encourages us to do. When we focus on these things, our minds are renewed, and we become more sensitive to the leading of the Holy Spirit.

Discernment also requires humility and a willingness to submit to God's will, even when it's not what we initially wanted or expected. Sometimes, God's will might be difficult to accept, especially if it involves sacrifice or going against the grain of what society expects. But true discernment means trusting that God's plans are better than our own, even when we don't fully understand them. It means believing that God's will is not only good and acceptable but also perfect—that is, it's exactly what we need, even if it's not always what we want. This kind of trust is built over time as we see God's faithfulness in our lives and learn to rely on His wisdom rather than our own understanding.

In addition to helping us make wise decisions, discernment also protects us from being deceived by false teachings or being led astray by those who do not have our best interests at heart. In a world where there are so many voices competing for our attention, discernment helps us to distinguish between what is true and what is false, what is helpful and what is harmful. This is especially important in our spiritual lives, where there are many ideas and teachings that may sound good on the surface but are actually contrary to God's Word. By renewing our minds and staying grounded in God's truth, we can recognize when something doesn't align with His Word and avoid being misled.

Discernment also plays a vital role in our relationships. It helps us to see people and situations through God's eyes, rather than just our own. This means being able to recognize when someone is in need of encouragement or support, or when a situation requires us to speak up for what is right, even if it's difficult. It also means being able to discern when to be patient and when to take action, when to forgive and when to set boundaries. In all these situations, discernment allows us to respond in a way that reflects God's love and wisdom, rather than just reacting based on our emotions or what others expect of us.

Moreover, discernment leads to a life that is marked by peace and confidence in God's guidance. When we know that we are walking in God's will, we can have peace, even in the midst of uncertainty or challenges. We don't have to worry about whether we're making the right decisions because we know that God is leading us. This doesn't mean that life will always be easy or that we won't face difficulties, but it does mean that we can trust that God is in control and that He is working all things together for our good. This assurance comes from a mind that has been renewed and is able to discern God's will.

In conclusion, Romans 12:1-2 teaches us the importance of discernment in the Christian life. Discernment is the ability to understand and act according to God's will, and it is essential for living a life that honors Him. By renewing our minds, we become better equipped to discern what is good, acceptable, and perfect in God's eyes. This involves immersing ourselves in God's Word, seeking His guidance, and being willing to submit to His will, even when it's challenging. Discernment protects us from being led astray by false teachings and helps us to navigate our relationships and decisions in a way that reflects God's wisdom and love. It leads to a life marked by peace and confidence in God's guidance, knowing that we are walking in His will. As we continue to renew our minds and grow in our ability to discern God's will, we can trust that He will guide us and help us to live lives that are pleasing to Him. This ongoing process of transformation and renewal is at the heart of what it means to live as a living sacrifice, holy and acceptable to God, and it is the foundation of true spiritual worship.

Chapter 4 – The Diligence

Romans 12:1-2 is a passage that teaches us about the importance of living a life that is fully dedicated to God, and one of the key concepts in these verses is diligence. Diligence means putting in consistent effort and being persistent in our tasks, especially when it comes to our spiritual growth. When Paul talks about being transformed by the renewing of our minds, he is not talking about something that happens automatically or overnight. This transformation requires hard work and commitment, and it involves a constant, ongoing effort to study God's Word and seek His guidance in every aspect of our lives. To understand what Paul is saying, we need to realize that our minds are constantly being influenced by the world around us. We are bombarded with messages from the media, our peers, and society that often go against what God teaches us in the Bible. These influences can shape our thinking in ways that are not aligned with God's will, leading us to make decisions that are more in line with worldly values than with God's truth. This is why it is so important for us to be diligent in renewing our minds through the study of God's Word. By doing this, we can begin to see the world from God's perspective and develop the discernment we need to live according to His will.

Studying God's Word is not something that we can do casually or occasionally if we want to experience true transformation. It requires a serious and sustained effort. This means setting aside regular time to read and meditate on the Scriptures, to pray, and to reflect on how God's Word applies to our lives. It also means being intentional about learning from others who are more mature in their faith, whether through Bible studies, sermons, or conversations with fellow believers. The more time we spend in God's Word, the more our minds will be renewed, and the more we will be able to understand and follow God's will for our lives. But this process is not always easy. There will be times when we feel discouraged, distracted, or even tempted to give up. This is where diligence comes in. Diligence means continuing to press on, even when it's difficult, trusting that God will reward our efforts and help us grow in our faith.

One of the reasons why diligence is so important in the process of renewing our minds is that we live in a world that is constantly trying to pull us away from God. The values of the world often stand in direct opposition to the values of God's Kingdom, and if we are not careful, we can easily be led astray. The world tells us to seek wealth, power, and pleasure, while God calls us to seek first His Kingdom and His righteousness. The world encourages us to be self-reliant and independent, while God calls us to depend on Him and to trust in His guidance. The world promotes a mentality of "looking out for number one," while God calls us to love our neighbors as ourselves and to put others' needs ahead of our own. To resist these worldly influences and stay focused on God's truth requires diligence. It means constantly checking our thoughts, attitudes, and actions against the standard of God's Word and being willing to make changes when we see that we are not living according to His will.

Diligence also involves being proactive in seeking God's guidance. This means not only reading the Bible but also actively applying its teachings to our lives. It means praying regularly, not just for our needs, but also for wisdom and discernment to understand God's will. It means being open to the leading of the Holy Spirit and being willing to follow wherever He leads, even when it's uncomfortable or goes against our natural inclinations. This kind of diligence requires humility and a willingness to admit when we are wrong or when we need to change.

It also requires perseverance, because the process of transformation is a lifelong journey, not a one-time event.

Another aspect of diligence is accountability. We are not meant to walk this journey alone, and having others to support and encourage us can make a big difference in our ability to stay diligent in our spiritual growth. This is why being part of a church community or a small group is so important. In these settings, we can share our struggles and successes, learn from others, and be held accountable for our commitments to study God's Word and seek His guidance. When we are diligent in surrounding ourselves with godly influences, we are more likely to stay on track and continue growing in our faith.

It's also important to recognize that diligence in renewing our minds is not just about what we do in our private times of study and prayer, but also about how we live our lives every day. Our thoughts, words, and actions should all reflect the transformation that is taking place within us. This means being mindful of what we allow into our minds—whether through what we watch, listen to, or read—and being intentional about filling our minds with things that are true, noble, right, pure, lovely, and admirable, as Philippians 4:8 encourages us to do. It also means being diligent in living out our faith in practical ways, such as serving others, standing up for what is right, and sharing the love of Christ with those around us.

Diligence in renewing our minds also involves a willingness to learn and grow. This means being teachable and open to correction, whether it comes from God's Word, the Holy Spirit, or other believers. It means being willing to admit when we don't know something and to seek out the answers we need. It also means being patient with ourselves and with the process, recognizing that transformation takes time and that we are all works in progress. But through it all, we can be confident that as we are diligent in studying God's Word and seeking His guidance, He will be faithful to complete the good work He has begun in us.

In conclusion, Romans 12:1-2 calls us to a life of diligence in our spiritual growth. Being transformed by the renewing of our minds is not something that happens passively or by accident; it requires a consistent and intentional effort to study God's Word, seek His guidance, and apply His truth to our lives. This diligence is essential for resisting the influences of the world and staying focused on God's will. It involves setting aside regular time for study and prayer, being proactive in seeking God's guidance, surrounding ourselves with godly influences, and living out our faith in practical ways. It also requires humility, perseverance, and a willingness to learn and grow. As we are diligent in these things, we will experience the transformation that Paul talks about in Romans 12:2, and we will be better equipped to live lives that are holy, acceptable to God, and in line with His perfect will. This transformation is not just for our own benefit, but for the glory of God and the advancement of His Kingdom. By being diligent in renewing our minds, we become more like Christ, and we are able to reflect His love, truth, and grace to a world that desperately needs it. As we continue on this journey of transformation, we can trust that God will be with us every step of the way, guiding us, strengthening us, and helping us to grow in our faith.

Chapter 5 – The Discipline

Romans 12:1-2 is a passage that challenges us to live a life of true commitment to God, and a key aspect of this commitment is discipline. Discipline is crucial when it comes to offering our bodies as a living sacrifice because it requires us to make constant, intentional choices that align with God's will rather than the patterns of the world. The world is full of temptations and distractions that can easily lead us away from the path God has set before us, which is why discipline is so important. To be disciplined means to have control over our desires, thoughts, and actions, ensuring that they are in line with what God wants for our lives. This passage urges us not to be conformed to this world, but to be transformed by the renewing of our minds. This transformation doesn't happen by accident; it requires a disciplined effort to resist the pull of worldly values and instead focus on what pleases God.

Offering our bodies as a living sacrifice is a call to give our whole selves to God, holding nothing back. This isn't just about what we do on Sundays at church or during our prayer time, but about how we live every day, in every moment. It means making choices that reflect our commitment to God, even when it's difficult or when it goes against what others around us are doing. For example, it might mean choosing honesty when lying would be easier, or showing kindness to someone who has wronged us. These choices require discipline because they often go against our natural inclinations and the pressures of the world. The world tells us to look out for ourselves, to pursue our own desires, and to conform to the values and behaviors of those around us. But as

Christians, we are called to a different standard—God's standard. This means we have to be disciplined in our thoughts, in what we allow into our minds, and in how we respond to the world around us.

Discipline in the Christian life is about more than just avoiding sin; it's about actively pursuing righteousness. It's about being intentional in our relationship with God, making time for prayer, Bible study, and worship, even when life gets busy. It's about being consistent in our walk with God, not just when we feel like it, but every day. This kind of discipline is not easy, but it is necessary if we want to live a life that is pleasing to God. It requires us to be aware of the influences in our lives and to make conscious decisions about what we allow to shape us. For instance, the media we consume, the people we spend time with, and the activities we engage in all have the potential to influence our thinking and behavior. If we are not disciplined in guarding our hearts and minds, we can easily be led astray by the world's values.

Paul's call to offer our bodies as a living sacrifice also speaks to the need for discipline in how we treat our bodies. This means recognizing that our bodies are temples of the Holy Spirit and should be treated with respect and care. It means being disciplined in our habits, such as eating, exercise, and rest, so that we can be healthy and able to serve God effectively. It also means being disciplined in our sexuality, honoring God with our bodies by living according to His standards of purity and holiness. This kind of discipline is countercultural in a world that often promotes indulgence and self-gratification, but it is essential for living a life that is set apart for God.

Furthermore, discipline in the Christian life involves the renewing of our minds, as mentioned in Romans 12:2. Our minds are like gardens; what we plant in them will grow and bear fruit, whether good or bad. If we allow the world's messages to take root in our minds, they will produce worldly attitudes and behaviors. But if we are disciplined in planting God's Word in our minds, it will produce godly attitudes and behaviors. This means being disciplined in our thought life, choosing to meditate on things that are true, noble, right, pure, lovely, and admirable, as Philippians 4:8 instructs us. It means being disciplined in rejecting thoughts that do not align with God's truth, such as thoughts of fear, doubt, or temptation, and replacing them with thoughts that are rooted in God's Word.

Discipline also plays a key role in our relationships. Offering our bodies as a living sacrifice means being disciplined in how we treat others, striving to love them as Christ loves us. This can be challenging, especially when others are difficult to love or when we are tempted to respond in anger or frustration. But discipline calls us to rise above these challenges and to respond with grace, patience, and kindness. It means being disciplined in our speech, choosing words that build up rather than tear down, and being disciplined in our actions, seeking to serve others selflessly rather than seeking our own gain.

One of the greatest challenges to discipline in the Christian life is the temptation to conform to the world's patterns. The world is constantly trying to shape us into its mold, whether through peer pressure, societal norms, or the desire for acceptance and approval. But as believers, we are called to be different, to stand out as lights in a dark world. This requires discipline because it often means going against the grain, making choices that are unpopular or countercultural. It means being willing to say no to things that others might say yes to, and being willing to stand firm in our convictions, even when it costs us something. This kind of discipline is not about being legalistic or self-righteous, but about being committed to living in a way that honors God.

Discipline is also necessary for persevering in the Christian life. The journey of faith is not always easy, and there will be times when we face trials, temptations, and challenges that test our commitment to God. In these moments, discipline is what keeps us going, helping us to stay focused on God's promises and to continue trusting Him, even when the road is hard. It's what helps us to keep praying, keep studying God's Word, and keep serving others, even when we don't see immediate results or when we feel like giving up. Discipline reminds us that the Christian life is a marathon, not a sprint, and that we need to pace ourselves, stay strong, and keep moving forward, one step at a time.

Moreover, discipline is not something we can muster up on our own; it is a fruit of the Spirit. As we walk in step with the Holy Spirit, He gives us the strength and self-control we need to live disciplined lives. This means that discipline is not just about our own efforts, but about relying on God's power at work within us. It's about surrendering to His leading, trusting Him to guide us, and allowing Him to shape us into the image of Christ. The more we depend on the Holy Spirit, the more disciplined we become, because we are no longer relying on our own strength, but on His.

In conclusion, Romans 12:1-2 calls us to a life of discipline in our walk with God. Offering our bodies as a living sacrifice demands discipline, as we must continually resist conforming to the world's patterns and instead be transformed by the renewing of our minds. Discipline is essential for maintaining a strong and growing relationship with God, for living a life that is pleasing to Him, and for persevering in our faith. It involves making intentional choices that reflect our commitment to God, guarding our hearts and minds, treating our bodies with respect, and loving others as Christ loves us. Discipline is not about trying to earn God's favor, but about responding to His grace by living in a way that honors Him. It is a daily decision to follow Jesus, to take up our cross, and to live for His glory. As we grow in discipline, we become more like Christ, and our lives become a testimony to the transforming power of God's love and grace. Discipline is not easy, but it is necessary for living a life that is set apart for God, and it is made possible by the power of the Holy Spirit working within us. As we commit ourselves to a life of discipline, we can trust that God will continue to work in us, renewing our minds, strengthening our hearts, and guiding us every step of the way.

Chapter 6 – The Direction

Romans 12:1-2 is a powerful passage that emphasizes the importance of allowing God to transform our minds so that we can live lives that are pleasing to Him. One of the key ideas in these verses is the concept of direction. Direction refers to the guidance we receive from God that helps us make decisions and take actions that align with His purpose for our lives. When we allow God to transform our minds, we are no longer conformed to the patterns of this world, which are often focused on self-interest, materialism, and temporary pleasures. Instead, we begin to see things from God's perspective and understand what is truly important. This transformation provides us with clear direction, helping us navigate the challenges and choices we face in life.

The process of transforming our minds begins with presenting our bodies as a living sacrifice to God, which is described in Romans 12:1 as our "reasonable service" or spiritual worship. This means that we are to dedicate every part of our being—our thoughts, desires, and actions—to God. By doing this, we open ourselves up to His guidance and direction. However, this transformation does not happen overnight. It requires a commitment to studying God's Word, seeking His guidance in prayer, and being open to the work of the Holy Spirit in our lives. As we immerse ourselves in God's truth, our minds are renewed, and we begin to think and act in ways that are aligned with His will.

One of the most significant benefits of this transformation is that it provides us with clear direction for our lives. In a world that is often confusing and chaotic, having a sense of direction is invaluable. When we are conformed to the world, we may find ourselves making decisions based on what seems right at the moment or what others expect of us. However, these decisions may not always lead to the best outcomes or fulfill God's purpose for our lives. By contrast, when our minds are transformed by God's truth, we are better equipped to discern what is the good, acceptable, and perfect will of God, as mentioned in Romans 12:2. This discernment helps us make choices that are in line with God's plan for us and that lead to true fulfillment and peace.

Having clear direction from God also means that we can avoid many of the pitfalls and traps that the world sets before us. The world often promotes values and behaviors that are contrary to God's will, such as selfishness, greed, and immorality. If we are not careful, we can easily be led astray by these influences and make decisions that bring us harm or lead us away from God. However, when our minds are renewed and we are following God's direction, we are able to see through these deceptions and make choices that honor Him. This doesn't mean that we will never face challenges or difficulties, but it does mean that we can approach these situations with confidence, knowing that we are following God's guidance.

Direction from God also helps us to live with purpose. Many people go through life feeling lost or unsure of what they are supposed to do. They may try different things, hoping to find something that brings them happiness or success, but often these pursuits end in disappointment. However, when we are following God's direction, we have a clear sense of purpose. We know that our lives have meaning and that we are here for a reason. This purpose gives us motivation and drive, helping us to stay focused on what is truly important and not be distracted by the things of the world.

Another important aspect of direction is that it helps us to prioritize our time and energy. There are countless things that can demand our attention, from work and family responsibilities to hobbies and social activities. While many of these things are good and important, it is easy to become overwhelmed or to spread ourselves too thin if we do not have a clear sense of direction. When we are following God's guidance, we are able to prioritize our activities in a way that reflects His will for our lives. This means that we can focus on the things that truly matter and that will have the most impact for God's Kingdom, rather than wasting time on things that are ultimately insignificant.

Direction from God also brings peace and confidence. When we are unsure of what to do or where to go, it is easy to become anxious or stressed. We may worry about making the wrong decision or fear that we will miss out on something important. However, when we are following God's direction, we can rest in the assurance that He is leading us and that He knows what is best for us. This peace allows us to move forward with confidence, even when the path ahead is uncertain or when we face obstacles. We can trust that God is in control and that He will provide for us and guide us every step of the way.

In addition to guiding our decisions and actions, direction from God also helps us to build strong and healthy relationships. When our minds are transformed by God's truth, we are better able to see others through His eyes and to treat them with love and respect. This means that we are more likely to make decisions that strengthen our relationships rather than harm them. For example, we may be more patient and understanding with others, more willing to forgive, and more committed to serving and supporting those around us. These qualities help us to build relationships that are based on mutual trust and respect, which are essential for a healthy and fulfilling life.

Direction from God also empowers us to fulfill the specific calling that He has for each of our lives. Every person has a unique role to play in God's Kingdom, and following His direction is essential for discovering and fulfilling that role. Whether it is in our careers, our families, our communities, or our churches, God has a plan for how we can use our gifts and talents to serve Him and make a difference in the world. When we are following His guidance, we are able to step into our calling with confidence and to make a meaningful impact for His glory.

Furthermore, direction from God helps us to persevere in the face of challenges and difficulties. Life is full of obstacles, and there will be times when we are tempted to give up or to take an easier path. However, when we have a clear sense of direction from God, we are able to stay focused on His purpose for us, even when the going gets tough. We know that He is with us and that He will provide the strength and resources we need to overcome whatever challenges we face. This perseverance is essential for achieving the goals that God has set before us and for living a life that is pleasing to Him.

In conclusion, Romans 12:1-2 teaches us the importance of allowing God to transform our minds so that we can receive clear direction for our lives. This direction is essential for making decisions and taking actions that are aligned with God's will and purpose. When we are following God's guidance, we are better equipped to navigate the challenges of life, to prioritize our time and energy, to build strong and healthy relationships, and to fulfill our unique calling in His Kingdom. Direction from God also brings peace and confidence, helping us to move forward with trust in His plan for us. As we continue to renew our minds through the study of God's Word and prayer, we can trust that He will provide the direction we need to live lives that are pleasing to Him and that bring glory to His name.

Chapter 7 – The Distinction

Romans 12:1-2 is a passage that speaks powerfully about the transformation that takes place in the life of a believer when they choose to live according to God's will rather than the ways of the world. One of the key concepts in these verses is the idea of distinction, which means being set apart or different from the world around us. The Bible tells us that as Christians, we are called to be in the world but not of the world, and Romans 12:1-2 highlights this by urging us not to conform to the world but to be transformed by the renewing of our minds. This distinction is crucial because it defines the difference between a life that is led by worldly standards and one that is guided by God. The world often promotes values and behaviors that are in direct opposition to what God desires for us, such as selfishness, materialism, and a focus on temporary pleasures. If we conform to these worldly standards, we may find ourselves living lives that are shallow, unfulfilling, and ultimately separated from God's purpose. However, when we choose to follow God's guidance and allow Him to transform our minds, we create a clear distinction between our lives and the lives of those who are led by the world.

This distinction is not just about outward behaviors but is rooted in the very way we think and perceive the world. When Paul talks about being transformed by the renewing of our minds, he is emphasizing the importance of letting God change the way we think, so that our thoughts align with His truth rather than the lies and deceptions of the world. This transformation leads to a life that is distinctly different from those who are driven by worldly desires. It's a life marked by love, humility, generosity, and a deep commitment to following God's will. This distinction is important not only for our own spiritual growth but also for our witness to others. When people see the difference in our lives, it can be a powerful testimony to the reality of God's presence and work within us. They may see the peace and joy that we have, even in difficult circumstances, and wonder what makes us different. This opens the door for us to share the gospel and to point others to the source of our hope and strength.

Living a life of distinction also means making choices that may not always be popular or easy. The world often pressures us to fit in, to go along with the crowd, and to adopt its standards and values. But as Christians, we are called to a higher standard, one that is set by God and not by the world. This can be challenging, especially when it means standing up for what is right in the face of opposition or criticism. It may mean making sacrifices or choosing a path that is less traveled, but the reward is a life that is pleasing to God and that reflects His glory. The distinction that comes from not conforming to the world also involves how we handle relationships, money, success, and power. The world's approach to these things often involves self-promotion, greed, and a desire for control. However, when we are guided by God's principles, we approach these areas of life with a heart of service, stewardship, and humility. We recognize that everything we have is a gift from God and that we are called to use it for His purposes, not just our own gain. This perspective sets us apart and creates a distinction that is evident to those around us.

Moreover, the distinction between a life led by worldly standards and one guided by God is also seen in our attitudes and responses to life's challenges. The world often responds to difficulty with fear, anger, or despair, but as believers, we are called to respond with faith, hope, and trust in God. This doesn't mean that we won't face struggles or that we won't feel the weight of difficult situations, but it does mean that we have a different foundation on which to stand. Our hope is not in the things of this world, which are temporary and uncertain, but in God, who is eternal and unchanging. This distinction is what gives us the strength to endure trials, to forgive those who wrong us, and to love our enemies. It's what enables us to find joy and contentment in all circumstances, knowing that our lives are in God's hands and that He is working all things for our good.

Another aspect of distinction is the way we view success and fulfillment. The world often measures success by wealth, power, status, and accomplishments. But God's definition of success is very different. He values faithfulness, obedience, and a heart that seeks to honor Him in all things. When we are guided by God's standards, we find our fulfillment not in what we achieve or acquire but in our relationship with Him and in living a life that reflects His love and grace. This creates a stark contrast between our lives and the lives of those who are chasing after the fleeting rewards of this world. Instead of striving for worldly success, we focus on growing in our faith, serving others, and building treasures in heaven that will last for eternity.

The distinction that comes from not conforming to the world also affects our sense of identity. The world often defines people by their achievements, appearance, or social status, but as believers, our identity is found in Christ. We are children of God, created in His image, and loved unconditionally by Him. This understanding of our identity shapes how we see ourselves and how we relate to others. It frees us from the need to compare ourselves to others or to seek validation from the world. Instead, we find our worth in who we are in Christ, and this gives us a sense of confidence and security that the world cannot offer. This distinction is especially important in a world that is increasingly focused on external appearances and superficial success. By grounding our identity in Christ, we can live with a sense of purpose and direction that is not dependent on the changing tides of worldly opinions or trends.

Living a life of distinction also means that we are set apart for God's purposes. This involves being holy, which means being dedicated to God and set apart from sin. The world often encourages behaviors and attitudes that are contrary to God's holiness, such as dishonesty, immorality, and selfishness. But as believers, we are called to be holy as God is holy. This means that we strive to live in a way that reflects God's character and that we avoid anything that would compromise our witness or dishonor Him. This pursuit of holiness creates a clear distinction between us and the world, as we seek to live lives that are pure, righteous, and pleasing to God.

Another important aspect of distinction is the way we handle time and priorities. The world often encourages us to live for the moment, to pursue pleasure and success at all costs, and to focus on our own goals and desires. But as believers, we are called to live with eternity in mind. This means that we prioritize our relationship with God, our spiritual growth, and our service to others over the temporary pleasures and pursuits of this world. We recognize that our time on earth is short and that we are called to use it wisely, making the most of every opportunity to glorify God and to make a difference for His Kingdom. This perspective sets us apart from the world and helps us to live with purpose and intention.

The distinction between a life led by worldly standards and one guided by God is also evident in our relationships with others. The world often promotes relationships based on convenience, mutual benefit, or self-interest. But as believers, we are called to love others sacrificially, to seek their good above our own, and to build relationships based on trust, respect, and mutual encouragement. This creates a community of believers that is distinct from the world, where people care for one another, support one another, and build each other up in love. This kind of community is a powerful witness to the world of the transforming power of the gospel and the love of Christ.

Finally, living a life of distinction means that we are always growing and changing, becoming more like Christ every day. This transformation is a lifelong process, and it requires us to continually seek God's guidance, to study His Word, and to be open to the work of the Holy Spirit in our lives. As we grow in our faith, the distinction between our lives and the lives of those who are led by the world becomes more and more evident. We begin to reflect more of God's character in our thoughts, words, and actions, and we become a living testimony to His grace and truth.

In conclusion, Romans 12:1-2 teaches us about the importance of living a life that is distinct from the world. This distinction is created by not conforming to the world's standards but by being transformed by the renewing of our minds. This transformation sets us apart and creates a clear contrast between a life led by worldly values and one guided by God's truth. This distinction is evident in every area of our lives, from our thoughts and attitudes to our relationships, priorities, and sense of identity. It's a distinction that not only helps us to live lives that are pleasing to God but also serves as a powerful witness to the world of the reality of God's presence and work within us. As we continue to seek God's guidance and allow Him to transform us, we can live lives that are set apart for His glory and that reflect His love and grace to a world that desperately needs it.

Chapter 8 – The Dedication

Romans 12:1-2 is a profound passage that calls us to a life of complete dedication to God, and this dedication is not just about performing religious duties or attending church services; it's about offering our entire selves as a living sacrifice to God, holding nothing back. This concept of dedication goes beyond just a momentary decision or a surface-level commitment—it involves a total and continuous surrender of our lives to God, in every aspect and in every moment. When Paul urges us to present our bodies as a living sacrifice, he is calling us to give up our own desires, our own plans, and even our own comforts, in order to fully embrace God's will for our lives. This kind of dedication is about more than just saying we believe in God; it's about living in a way that reflects that belief in every action we take, every word we speak, and every thought we entertain.

To dedicate our lives to God in the way that Romans 12:1-2 describes means that we must be willing to let go of anything that hinders our relationship with Him. This might include letting go of certain habits, behaviors, or even relationships that pull us away from God's purpose for our lives. It might mean making sacrifices in our careers, our finances, or our personal ambitions in order to follow the path that God has laid out for us. This kind of dedication requires a deep trust in God, believing that His plans for us are better than anything we could plan for ourselves, even when it's hard to see or understand at the moment. It means trusting that God knows what is best for us, and that He is working all things together for our good, even when the road is difficult or uncertain.

This call to dedication is also a call to holiness. Paul describes this living sacrifice as "holy, acceptable unto God," which means that our lives should be set apart for God's purposes, and free from the stain of sin. This doesn't mean that we will be perfect, but it does mean that we should strive to live in a way that honors God and reflects His character. It means being intentional about the choices we make, ensuring that they align with God's commands and His will for our lives. This kind of holiness requires daily surrender, a daily choice to die to our own desires and to live for God. It requires us to be vigilant in guarding our hearts and minds against the influences of the world that seek to pull us away from God's truth.

In addition to being holy, our dedication to God should be complete. Paul's use of the word "living" in describing the sacrifice implies that this is not a one-time event, but an ongoing, continuous offering of ourselves to God. It's easy to be dedicated to God in the moments when we feel strong or when everything is going well, but true dedication is about staying committed to God even when it's hard, even when we face trials, temptations, or doubts. It means continuing to follow God, even when the path He has called us to walk is difficult or when we don't understand why things are happening the way they are. This kind of dedication is about perseverance—it's about holding fast to our faith and our commitment to God, no matter what.

Moreover, dedication to God as described in Romans 12:1-2 is not just about what we do, but about who we are. It's about allowing God to transform us from the inside out, so that our lives reflect His love, His grace, and His truth in everything we do. Paul goes on to say in verse 2 that we should not be conformed to this world, but be transformed by the renewing of our minds. This transformation is a key part of our dedication to God because it's what enables us to live in a way that is pleasing to Him. It's what helps us to discern His will and to follow it faithfully. This transformation is not something that happens overnight, but it's a process that takes time, patience, and a willingness to let God work in our lives. It requires us to be open to the leading of the Holy Spirit, to be willing to change and to grow, and to be committed to becoming more like Christ every day.

Dedication to God also involves a deep sense of gratitude. Paul begins Romans 12:1 by saying, "I beseech you therefore, brethren, by the mercies of God." This phrase reminds us that our dedication to God is a response to His incredible mercy and grace in our lives. God has given us everything—our lives, our salvation, His love, and His promises—and our response to that should be one of wholehearted dedication. When we truly understand the depth of God's love for us and the magnitude of what He has done for us, our natural response should be to give our lives back to Him, holding nothing back. This dedication is not about trying to earn God's favor or love—that has already been given to us freely—but it's about responding to that love with a life that is fully committed to Him.

Another important aspect of dedication is that it requires discipline. Living as a living sacrifice means that we must be disciplined in our spiritual lives, making time for prayer, for reading and meditating on God's Word, and for worship. It means being disciplined in how we live our lives, making choices that reflect our commitment to God rather than the desires of the flesh or the pressures of the world. It means being disciplined in our relationships, treating others with love, respect, and kindness, even when it's difficult. This kind of discipline is not easy, but it's essential for living a life that is dedicated to God.

Dedication also involves service. When we offer our bodies as a living sacrifice, we are offering all that we are to God's service. This means that our lives should be characterized by a willingness to serve others, to put their needs ahead of our own, and to use our gifts and talents to further God's Kingdom. Service is a natural outflow of a life that is dedicated to God, because when we are truly committed to Him, we will want to share His love with others and to be a blessing to those around us. This service might take many forms, from helping those in need, to sharing the gospel, to simply being a source of encouragement and support to those around us. Whatever form it takes, service is an essential part of our dedication to God.

Furthermore, dedication to God as described in Romans 12:1-2 is something that affects every area of our lives. It's not just about our spiritual lives, but about our relationships, our work, our finances, and our daily choices. When we dedicate our lives to God, we are saying that He is Lord over every aspect of our lives, and that we are willing to follow Him in everything. This means that our dedication should be evident in how we treat others, in how we use our resources, and in how we conduct ourselves in our work and daily activities. It means living with integrity, honesty, and humility, knowing that everything we do is a reflection of our commitment to God.

Dedication also means being willing to stand out and be different. Paul warns us not to be conformed to this world, and this means that our dedication to God will often put us at odds with the world around us. The world may not understand or appreciate our commitment to God, and there may be times when we face opposition, criticism, or even persecution because of our faith. But true dedication means being willing to stand firm in our faith, even when it's difficult, and even when it means standing alone. It means being willing to be different, to be set apart, and to live in a way that is pleasing to God, even if it means going against the grain of the culture or the expectations of those around us.

Finally, dedication to God as described in Romans 12:1-2 is something that brings great joy and fulfillment. While it may involve sacrifice and discipline, it also brings us into a deeper relationship with God, where we experience His love, His peace, and His presence in a powerful way. When we live lives that are fully dedicated to God, we find that we are no longer chasing after the empty promises of the world, but are instead living in the fullness of God's purpose and plan for our lives. This brings a sense of joy and fulfillment that nothing else can offer. It's a joy that comes from knowing that we are living in the center of God's will, that we are being used by Him to make a difference in the world, and that we are growing in our relationship with Him every day.

In conclusion, Romans 12:1-2 calls us to a life of complete dedication to God, holding nothing back. This dedication involves offering our entire selves as a living sacrifice to God, allowing Him to transform us from the inside out, and living in a way that reflects His will and His character in every area of our lives. It requires us to be holy, disciplined, and willing to serve others, and it means being willing to stand firm in our faith, even when it's difficult. But this dedication is also something that brings great joy and fulfillment, as it brings us into a deeper relationship with God and allows us to live in the fullness of His purpose and plan for our lives. As we continue to dedicate our lives to God, we can trust that He will work in us, transforming us, guiding us, and using us for His glory.

Chapter 9 – The Dependence

Romans 12:1-2 is a deeply significant passage that teaches us about the nature of true Christian living, emphasizing the importance of depending fully on God's mercy and grace. One of the most profound lessons from these verses is the concept of dependence—understanding that our transformation, our ability to live as God desires, and our capacity to offer ourselves as living sacrifices are all rooted in God's power, not our own. This dependence on God is fundamental to the Christian life because it acknowledges that without God's mercy and grace, we are incapable of becoming who He calls us to be. When Paul urges us to present our bodies as a living sacrifice, holy and acceptable to God, which is our reasonable service, he is not suggesting that we can do this by sheer willpower or personal strength. Instead, he is pointing to the fact that it is only through God's mercy—His unearned favor and kindness—that we can even begin to offer ourselves to Him in such a way. This mercy is not something we can earn or deserve; it is a gift from God, freely given because of His love for us. Recognizing this is the first step in understanding our complete dependence on God.

Dependence on God is crucial because it shifts our focus from our own abilities, achievements, and efforts to God's strength, grace, and provision. Often, we are tempted to rely on our own understanding, to try to live out our faith by following rules, performing good deeds, or striving to be morally upright. While these things are important, they can never be the foundation of our transformation. True transformation—the kind that Paul talks about in Romans 12:2, where we are not conformed to this world but are transformed by the renewing of our minds—comes only through the power of the Holy Spirit working within us. It is God who changes our hearts, who renews our minds, and who enables us to live in a way that is pleasing to Him. Our role is to submit to Him, to depend on His grace, and to trust in His ability to do in us what we cannot do for ourselves.

This dependence is not a one-time decision but an ongoing, daily reliance on God. Every day, we are faced with choices, temptations, and challenges that test our commitment to live as living sacrifices. Without God's help, we would quickly fall back into the patterns of the world, conforming to its values and ways of thinking. But when we depend on God, we find that He gives us the strength to resist these temptations, the wisdom to discern His will, and the power to live according to His truth. This is why prayer is such an essential part of the Christian life. Through prayer, we acknowledge our dependence on God, we seek His guidance, and we ask for His help in living out our faith. Prayer is a way of humbling ourselves before God, recognizing that we need Him in every aspect of our lives.

Moreover, dependence on God's mercy and grace reminds us that our worth and identity are not based on our performance or accomplishments but on what Christ has done for us. The world often measures value by success, wealth, status, or achievements, but in God's kingdom, our worth is found in the fact that we are loved by God and redeemed by Christ's sacrifice on the cross. This truth liberates us from the pressure to prove ourselves or to earn God's favor through our own efforts. Instead, we can rest in the assurance that we are accepted by God because of His mercy, and that He is at work in us, transforming us into the image of His Son. This understanding of dependence fosters humility, as we recognize that everything we have, and everything we are, is a result of God's grace.

Dependence on God also means trusting Him in the process of transformation, even when it's difficult or when we don't see immediate results. Transformation is not an instant change but a lifelong journey of becoming more like Christ. There will be times when we struggle, when we fail, or when we feel like we are not making progress. In these moments, it's easy to become discouraged or to doubt whether we will ever truly change. But dependence on God means believing that He is faithful to complete the good work He has begun in us, as Philippians 1:6 assures us. It means trusting that God's grace is sufficient for us, and that His power is made perfect in our weakness, as Paul reminds us in 2 Corinthians 12:9. This dependence gives us the perseverance to keep going, to keep trusting God, and to keep submitting to His work in our lives, even when the process is slow or painful.

Another aspect of dependence on God's mercy and grace is recognizing that we cannot live the Christian life alone. We need the support, encouragement, and accountability of other believers. The church is not just a place where we go to worship; it's a community where we can grow together in our faith, share our struggles, and help one another live out the call to be living sacrifices. Dependence on God means being open to receiving help from others, being willing to admit our weaknesses, and being humble enough to ask for prayer and support when we need it. It also means being willing to offer that same support to others, recognizing that we are all in this journey together, and that God often works through the relationships we have with other believers to strengthen and encourage us.

Dependence on God also affects how we approach the challenges and difficulties of life. The world often tells us to rely on our own strength, to push through hardships with determination and self-reliance. But as Christians, we are called to a different way of living. When we face trials, we are to depend on God, trusting that He will give us the strength and grace we need to endure. This doesn't mean that we are passive or that we don't take action when necessary, but it does mean that our confidence is in God, not in ourselves. We look to Him for wisdom, for guidance, and for the resources we need to navigate the challenges of life. This dependence allows us to face difficulties with peace, knowing that God is with us, that He is in control, and that He will work all things together for our good, as Romans 8:28 promises.

Dependence on God also frees us from the fear of failure. When we are relying on our own strength, failure can be devastating, because it challenges our sense of self-worth and our confidence in our abilities. But when we are depending on God, we can face failure with grace, knowing that our identity is not tied to our successes or failures, but to who we are in Christ. We can learn from our mistakes, grow through our struggles, and trust that God is using even our failures to teach us, to refine us, and to draw us closer to Him. This dependence allows us to take risks in our faith, to step out in obedience to God's calling, even when we are unsure of the outcome, because we know that God is with us and that He will provide what we need.

Dependence on God's mercy and grace also brings us into a deeper relationship with Him. As we rely on Him, we experience His presence, His love, and His faithfulness in new and profound ways. We begin to see how He is at work in our lives, guiding us, providing for us, and shaping us into the people He created us to be. This deepens our trust in Him, strengthens our faith, and fills us with gratitude for His unending grace. Dependence on God is not a burden, but a source of joy and peace, because it connects us to the One who is all-powerful, all-knowing, and ever-loving. It reminds us that we are not alone, that we are cared for by a loving Father who delights in helping His children.

In conclusion, Romans 12:1-2 calls us to a life of complete dependence on God's mercy and grace. This passage teaches us that our transformation, our ability to live as living sacrifices, and our capacity to resist conforming to the world's patterns are all made possible through God's power, not our own. Dependence on God is foundational to the Christian life because it acknowledges that we are utterly reliant on His grace for everything we need. This dependence shifts our focus from our own efforts to God's strength, fostering humility, perseverance, and trust. It frees us from the fear of failure, liberates us from the pressure to prove ourselves, and brings us into a deeper relationship with God. As we continue to depend on Him, we find that He is faithful to transform us, to guide us, and to use us for His glory. Our role is to surrender to Him, to trust in His grace, and to rely on His power to live out the call to be living sacrifices, holy and acceptable to Him.

Chapter 10 – The Deference

Romans 12:1-2 is a profound passage that speaks to the heart of Christian living, calling us to offer our bodies as a living sacrifice and to be transformed by the renewing of our minds. One of the key lessons from these verses is the concept of deference, which involves submitting our desires to God's will and prioritizing His ways over our own. Deference, in this context, means recognizing that God's wisdom, plans, and purposes are far greater than anything we could imagine or achieve on our own. It's about acknowledging that, as humans, we are limited in our understanding, prone to selfishness, and often led astray by our own desires. In contrast, God's will is perfect, good, and aligned with what is truly best for us and the world around us. Therefore, deference requires us to willingly set aside our own agendas, ambitions, and even our personal preferences, in order to follow God's direction for our lives. This act of submission is not one of reluctance or defeat, but rather a joyful surrender to the one who knows us best and loves us most.

When Paul urges us to present our bodies as a living sacrifice, he is calling us to a life of complete dedication to God, where every aspect of who we are—our thoughts, emotions, actions, and desires—is offered up to God as an act of worship. This kind of dedication is not merely about outward conformity or religious rituals; it is about an inner transformation that affects the very core of our being. The phrase "living sacrifice" implies that this offering is ongoing, continuous, and involves our whole life. It is not a one-time event, but a daily decision to live in a way that honors God and reflects His character. To live as a living sacrifice means that we are willing to let go of our own plans and submit to God's will, even when it's difficult or when we don't fully understand what He is doing. This is where the concept of deference comes into play—choosing to prioritize God's will over our own requires a renewed mind that is continually being shaped by God's Word and His Spirit.

A renewed mind is central to living a life of deference because it changes the way we think about everything—our goals, our relationships, our challenges, and our purpose in life. When our minds are renewed, we begin to see things from God's perspective rather than from a purely human or worldly viewpoint. This transformation allows us to discern what is the good, acceptable, and perfect will of God, as Paul mentions in Romans 12:2. Discernment is crucial because it enables us to distinguish between what is temporary and fleeting versus what is eternal and significant. With a renewed mind, we start to value what God values and to desire what He desires. This shift in perspective is what leads us to deference—willingly submitting our desires to God's will because we trust that His ways are higher and better than our own.

Deference also involves humility, which is essential in the Christian life. Humility is recognizing that we are not the center of the universe, and that our lives are not primarily about fulfilling our own dreams and ambitions. Instead, our lives are about fulfilling God's purposes and bringing glory to Him. This requires us to take a step back, to quiet our own voices, and to listen for God's guidance. It means being willing to say, "Not my will, but Yours be done," even when our will seems strong or when the path God is leading us down seems uncertain or challenging. Humility allows us to accept that we don't always know what is best, and that we need God's wisdom and direction in every area of our lives. This is a radical departure from the mindset of the world, which often promotes self-reliance, self-promotion, and the pursuit of personal success above all else. Deference, on the other hand, is about putting God first, seeking His kingdom, and trusting that He will take care of the rest.

Moreover, deference is not about passivity or resignation; it is an active choice to align our lives with God's will. It requires intentionality and a daily commitment to seek God's guidance in all things. This might mean spending more time in prayer, reading and meditating on Scripture, or seeking counsel from mature believers who can help us discern God's will. It also means being open to the leading of the Holy Spirit, who often guides us in ways that are unexpected or contrary to our own plans. The Holy Spirit works in us to change our desires, to soften our hearts, and to give us a deeper love for God and for others. As we grow in our relationship with God, we become more attuned to His voice and more willing to follow where He leads, even if it means letting go of something we once held dear.

Deference also plays a crucial role in how we interact with others. When we submit our desires to God's will, we are better able to serve and love others in the way that God intends. We become less focused on our own needs and more focused on the needs of those around us. This is especially important in relationships, where selfishness and pride can often create conflict and division. By practicing deference, we learn to put others' needs ahead of our own, to listen more and speak less, and to seek reconciliation and peace rather than insisting on our own way. This kind of selfless love is a reflection of Christ's love for us, and it is a powerful testimony to the world of what it means to live a life that is surrendered to God.

Another aspect of deference is trust. To defer to God's will means to trust that He knows what is best for us, even when we don't understand why things are happening the way they are. This trust is built on the foundation of God's character—His goodness, faithfulness, and love. When we trust God, we can let go of the need to control our circumstances and outcomes, knowing that He is in control and that He is working all things together for our good. This doesn't mean that life will always be easy or that we won't face challenges, but it does mean that we can have peace in the midst of uncertainty, knowing that God is with us and that He is guiding our steps. This trust leads to a deeper sense of security and contentment, as we rest in the knowledge that God's plans for us are good, and that He is faithful to fulfill His promises.

Deference also brings freedom. When we submit our desires to God's will, we are freed from the burden of trying to figure everything out on our own. We no longer have to carry the weight of making sure our lives turn out exactly as we planned, because we trust that God is in control and that He will lead us where we need to go. This freedom allows us to live with a sense of joy and peace, knowing that our lives are in God's hands and that He is working in us and through us for His glory. It also frees us from the pressure to conform to the expectations of others or to chase after the fleeting pleasures of this world. Instead, we can focus on what truly matters—loving God, loving others, and living a life that reflects His character and His grace.

In conclusion, Romans 12:1-2 teaches us the importance of deference—submitting our desires to God's will and prioritizing His ways over our own. This passage calls us to a life of complete dedication to God, where we offer our bodies as a living sacrifice and are transformed by the renewing of our minds. Deference is a key aspect of this transformation, as it requires us to recognize that God's will is perfect, good, and far greater than anything we could achieve on our own. It involves humility, trust, and a willingness to let go of our own plans in order to follow God's direction for our lives. Deference also plays a crucial role in our relationships, as it enables us to love and serve others in the way that God intends. As we practice deference, we experience the freedom, peace, and joy that come from living a life that is fully surrendered to God. This kind of life is not easy, and it requires a daily commitment to seek God's will and to align our desires with His, but it is a life that brings true fulfillment and reflects the character of Christ to the world around us. As we continue to grow in our relationship with God, may we learn to defer to His will in all things, trusting that His plans for us are good, and that He is faithful to lead us on the path of life.

Chapter 11 – The Determination

Romans 12:1-2 is a powerful passage that calls believers to a life of true dedication to God, emphasizing the importance of transformation through the renewing of our minds. This transformation is not something that happens automatically or effortlessly; it requires determination—a steadfast, ongoing commitment to resist the influences of the world and to align our lives with God's principles. Determination, in this context, means having a strong resolve to live according to God's will, even when it's difficult, inconvenient, or goes against the grain of society. The world is constantly trying to shape our thoughts, values, and behaviors to fit its mold, which often leads us away from the truth and righteousness that God desires for us. However, Paul's instruction in Romans 12:2, "And be not conformed to this world: but be ye transformed by the renewing of your mind," reminds us that as Christians, we are called to be different—to live lives that reflect God's standards rather than the world's. This requires a determined effort to renew our minds daily with God's Word, to seek His guidance, and to make choices that honor Him.

Determination is crucial because the path of transformation is not easy. It involves a constant battle between the flesh and the spirit, between our natural inclinations and the desires of God. The world offers many temptations that appeal to our flesh—things like materialism, pride, selfishness, and the pursuit of pleasure—while God calls us to a life of humility, selflessness, and holiness. To resist these worldly influences, we must be determined to stand firm in our faith, even when we are surrounded by messages that encourage us to compromise our beliefs or to take the easy way out. This determination is not just about willpower; it is about relying on the strength that God provides through His Holy Spirit. As we draw closer to God, He gives us the power to overcome the temptations and pressures of the world, enabling us to live in a way that is pleasing to Him.

Living a transformed life also requires determination because it often involves going against the current of popular culture. The world has its own set of values and norms that are often contrary to what God teaches us in the Bible. For example, the world may glorify success, wealth, and power, while God values humility, service, and love. The world may promote a "me-first" mentality, encouraging us to prioritize our own desires and ambitions, while God calls us to put others before ourselves and to seek His Kingdom above all else. To live according to God's principles in such a culture requires determination because it means being willing to be different, to stand out, and sometimes even to face criticism or rejection for our faith. This determination is rooted in a deep conviction that God's ways are better, that His truth is unchanging, and that His promises are worth any sacrifice we may have to make.

Another aspect of determination is perseverance. Transformation is not a one-time event; it is a lifelong process of becoming more like Christ. This process involves daily choices, small and large, that shape our character and draw us closer to God. There will be times when we feel discouraged, when we fail, or when it seems like the changes we desire are happening too slowly. In these moments, determination is what keeps us going. It's what helps us to get back up when we fall, to keep seeking God's will, and to trust that He is at work in us, even when we can't see it. Determination means not giving up, even when the journey is hard, and trusting that God's grace is sufficient to carry us through.

Determination also requires discipline. To resist worldly influences and align with God's principles, we must be disciplined in our spiritual practices, such as prayer, Bible study, and worship. These practices help to renew our minds and to keep us focused on God's truth. They remind us of who God is, what He has done for us, and what He requires of us as His children. Discipline also involves making intentional choices about what we allow into our minds and hearts—whether it's the media we consume, the people we spend time with, or the thoughts we entertain. By being disciplined in these areas, we create an environment that supports our spiritual growth and helps us to stay aligned with God's will. This kind of discipline is not always easy, but it is essential for maintaining a close relationship with God and for living a life that is set apart for His purposes.

Moreover, determination in the Christian life involves a commitment to growth and change. God is always calling us to grow, to deepen our faith, and to become more like Christ. This growth often requires us to step out of our comfort zones, to confront areas of sin in our lives, and to be open to the refining work of the Holy Spirit. It requires us to be teachable, to listen to God's correction, and to be willing to make changes in our attitudes, behaviors, and priorities. This process of growth can be uncomfortable, and it can be tempting to resist or to settle for where we are. But determination means embracing the process, trusting that God's work in us is good, and being willing to go wherever He leads, even when it's difficult or when it requires sacrifice.

Determination also involves a reliance on community. God never intended for us to walk the path of transformation alone. He has given us the church—a community of believers who can support, encourage, and hold us accountable as we seek to live out our faith. Being part of a community requires determination because it means committing to relationships, being vulnerable, and allowing others to speak into our lives. It means being willing to give and receive help, to share our struggles and successes, and to be there for others as they walk their own journeys of transformation. In community, we find strength, wisdom, and encouragement that help us to stay determined in our pursuit of God's will.

Furthermore, determination is fueled by hope. As Christians, our determination is not based on wishful thinking or blind optimism; it is grounded in the hope that we have in Christ. This hope assures us that our efforts to live according to God's principles are not in vain, that God is with us, and that He is working all things together for our good. It reminds us that there is a future reward awaiting us—a crown of righteousness that the Lord will give to those who have faithfully followed Him. This hope gives us the strength to persevere, to keep fighting the good fight, and to stay committed to the process of transformation, knowing that in the end, it will all be worth it.

Finally, determination requires us to keep our eyes on Jesus. He is the author and perfecter of our faith, the one who began a good work in us and who will carry it on to completion. As we look to Jesus, we find the perfect example of determination—He endured the cross, despising its shame, for the joy set before Him. He remained steadfast in His mission, even when it meant suffering and death, because He was determined to do the will of His Father and to save us from our sins. In the same way, we are called to follow His example, to take up our cross daily, and to remain determined in our commitment to God's will, no matter what challenges we face.

In conclusion, Romans 12:1-2 calls us to a life of determination—a steadfast commitment to resist the influences of the world and to align our lives with God's principles. This determination is essential for the process of transformation, which is a lifelong journey of becoming more like Christ. It involves perseverance, discipline, growth, community, hope, and a focus on Jesus. As we remain determined in our pursuit of God's will, we will experience the renewing of our minds, the transformation of our hearts, and the fulfillment of God's good, acceptable, and perfect plan for our lives. This determination is not something we muster up on our own; it is fueled by the grace and strength that God provides through His Holy Spirit. As we depend on Him, we can be confident that He will give us the power to live as living sacrifices, holy and acceptable to Him, and to walk in the fullness of His purposes for us. May we, with determined hearts, continue to seek God's will, to resist the temptations of the world, and to live lives that bring glory and honor to His name.

Chapter 12 – The Delight

Romans 12:1-2 is a passage that speaks deeply to the heart of what it means to live a life dedicated to God. These verses call us to offer ourselves as living sacrifices, which is our reasonable service, and to be transformed by the renewing of our minds so that we can prove what is the good, acceptable, and perfect will of God. The process of offering ourselves to God and allowing Him to transform our minds is not just about duty or obligation; it leads to something much more profound and beautiful—it leads to delight. The ultimate result of living in this way is finding true joy and fulfillment in God's will and purpose for our lives. Delight, in this context, is not merely a fleeting emotion or temporary happiness; it is a deep, abiding sense of satisfaction and contentment that comes from living in alignment with God's will.

To understand this delight, we must first grasp the significance of offering ourselves as living sacrifices. When Paul speaks of presenting our bodies as a living sacrifice, he is calling us to a total commitment to God—one that involves every part of our lives. This kind of sacrifice is living, meaning it is ongoing and active. It's not a one-time act but a continual surrender of our desires, plans, and will to God. This surrender can be challenging because it requires us to let go of our own ambitions and to trust that God's plans for us are better than anything we could plan for ourselves. However, as we make this sacrifice, something incredible happens: we begin to experience a deep sense of peace and joy that comes from knowing we are living in God's will. This is the beginning of true delight.

The transformation that comes from renewing our minds is also central to experiencing this delight. The world is constantly trying to shape our thoughts and values in ways that often lead us away from God's truth. However, when we allow God to renew our minds, He changes the way we think, perceive, and understand the world. We start to see things from His perspective, and our desires begin to align with His. This renewal is not just about gaining knowledge or understanding more about God's will; it's about a complete transformation of our inner being that leads to a life of true joy and fulfillment. As our minds are renewed, we begin to delight in God's will because we recognize that His ways are perfect, His plans are good, and His purposes bring us the deepest satisfaction.

Delight in God's will is something that grows over time as we continue to walk with Him. Initially, the idea of surrendering our will to God might seem difficult or even daunting. We might worry that following God's plan means giving up things we enjoy or missing out on what the world has to offer. But as we take steps of faith and begin to experience the goodness of God's will, we discover that what He offers us is far greater than anything we could have imagined. We find that the things we once thought were important pale in comparison to the joy of living in God's purpose. This realization leads to a deepening delight in His will, as we come to understand that true joy and fulfillment are found not in pursuing our own desires, but in aligning our lives with God's eternal purposes.

Another aspect of delight is the sense of purpose and meaning that comes from living according to God's will. The world often promotes a pursuit of success, wealth, and pleasure as the path to happiness, but these things are ultimately empty and unsatisfying. In contrast, living for God's purpose gives our lives true significance. We find joy in knowing that we are part of something bigger than ourselves, that our lives have eternal value, and that we are making a difference in the world for God's Kingdom. This sense of purpose is deeply fulfilling because it connects us to God's greater plan for humanity and gives us a reason to live that goes beyond our own personal gain.

Delight in God's will also brings a profound sense of peace. When we are aligned with God's purposes, we no longer have to worry about the future or strive anxiously to control our circumstances. We can rest in the knowledge that God is in control, that He is guiding our steps, and that He is working all things together for our good. This peace is not dependent on our circumstances but comes from a deep trust in God's sovereignty and His goodness. It allows us to face challenges with confidence, knowing that God is with us and that He will provide everything we need. This peace, combined with the joy of living in God's will, creates a sense of delight that sustains us even in the midst of difficulties.

Delight in God's will also transforms our relationships. When we are living in alignment with God's purposes, we become more loving, patient, and kind, reflecting the character of Christ to those around us. Our relationships are enriched because they are no longer based on selfish desires or needs, but on a genuine desire to love and serve others as Christ loves us. This leads to deeper, more meaningful connections with others, which in turn brings us greater joy and fulfillment. We find delight in the way God uses us to bless others, and in the ways He brings people into our lives to encourage and support us.

Moreover, delight in God's will leads to a life of worship. When we recognize the goodness of God's plans and experience the joy of living in His purpose, our natural response is to worship Him. Worship becomes more than just singing songs or attending church services; it becomes a way of life. Every act of obedience, every step of faith, and every moment of surrender becomes an expression of our love and gratitude to God. This lifestyle of worship is deeply satisfying because it connects us to the source of all joy—God Himself. As we worship Him, we experience His presence in a profound way, and our delight in Him grows even deeper.

Delight in God's will also equips us to handle trials and difficulties with grace. When we are secure in the knowledge that we are living in God's purpose, we are better able to trust Him in the midst of challenges. We understand that even our trials have a purpose in God's plan and that He is using them to shape us, strengthen our faith, and draw us closer to Him. This perspective allows us to find joy even in the midst of suffering because we know that God is with us, that He is using our struggles for our good, and that He will bring us through to a place of greater strength and maturity. This joy in the midst of trials is a powerful testimony to the world of the transforming power of God's grace.

Furthermore, delight in God's will produces a deep sense of gratitude. As we see God's hand at work in our lives and experience the blessings of living according to His purpose, our hearts are filled with thankfulness. We become more aware of God's goodness, His faithfulness, and His constant provision. This gratitude fuels our delight in Him and strengthens our resolve to continue living in His will. It also changes our perspective on life, helping us to see even the small, everyday moments as gifts from God. This attitude of gratitude enhances our joy and makes every day an opportunity to celebrate God's goodness.

In addition, delight in God's will gives us a sense of identity and belonging. When we offer ourselves as living sacrifices and allow God to renew our minds, we come to understand who we truly are in Christ. We are no longer defined by the world's standards or by our own achievements, but by our relationship with God. We find our identity in being His beloved children, chosen and called for His purposes. This identity gives us a sense of security and confidence, knowing that we are loved and valued by God. It also gives us a sense of belonging, as we realize that we are part of God's family, connected to Him and to other believers in a deep and meaningful way. This sense of identity and belonging adds to our delight, as we rest in the assurance that we are exactly where we are meant to be—in the center of God's will.

Finally, delight in God's will leads to a life of fruitfulness. As we live according to God's purpose, we begin to see the fruit of His Spirit manifested in our lives—love, joy, peace, patience, kindness, goodness, faithfulness, gentleness, and self-control. These qualities not only bring us personal fulfillment but also have a positive impact on those around us. Our lives become a testimony to the power of God's transforming grace, and we become vessels through which His love and truth can flow to others. This fruitfulness brings us deep joy because it reflects the work of God in and through us. It is the fulfillment of Jesus' promise in John 15:11, where He says, "These things have I spoken unto you, that my joy might remain in you, and that your joy might be full." Living in God's will not only brings us joy but also makes our lives a source of joy and blessing to others.

In conclusion, Romans 12:1-2 calls us to a life of offering ourselves as living sacrifices and being transformed by the renewing of our minds. The ultimate result of living this way is delight—finding true joy and fulfillment in God's will and purpose for our lives. This delight is not just a fleeting emotion but a deep, abiding sense of satisfaction that comes from knowing we are living in alignment with God's perfect plan. It brings us peace, purpose, and a sense of identity, and it enriches our relationships, equips us to handle trials, and leads to a life of worship and fruitfulness. As we continue to surrender our lives to God and allow Him to transform us, we will experience the fullness of His joy, and our lives will become a reflection of His goodness and grace to the world around us. May we all seek to live in this delight, trusting that God's will is not only good and acceptable but also the source of our greatest joy and fulfillment.

Conclusion

As we draw to the close of "Living for God: The Call to Be a Living Sacrifice," the journey we have embarked on together is far from over. Instead, it is the beginning of a lifelong pursuit of living fully for God, embracing the call to be a living sacrifice as outlined in Romans 12:1-2. Throughout these pages, we have explored the depth of what it means to offer ourselves wholly to God—not just in moments of religious devotion, but in every aspect of our daily lives. This call to be a living sacrifice is a radical invitation to let go of our own desires, to resist the conforming pressures of the world, and to allow our minds and hearts to be transformed by God's truth. It's about living with purpose, direction, and a deep sense of joy that comes from knowing we are aligned with God's perfect will. The challenge now lies in taking these truths and applying them, making them the foundation upon which we build our lives. The journey of living for God is not easy; it requires perseverance, discipline, and above all, a relentless determination to pursue God's heart above all else. But it is also a journey filled with profound rewards—peace that surpasses understanding, a deep and abiding joy, and the fulfillment that comes from knowing you are living out the purpose for which you were created. As you close this book, may you be inspired and empowered to continue walking this path of transformation, allowing God to use your life as a living testimony to His grace and power. Remember, the call to be a living sacrifice is not just a call to sacrifice, but a call to live—to live fully, purposefully, and joyfully for the glory of God. May your life be a beacon of His love, shining brightly in a world that so desperately needs His light.

Don't miss out!

Visit the website below and you can sign up to receive emails whenever Joshua Rhoades publishes a new book. There's no charge and no obligation.

https://books2read.com/r/B-A-AJLBB-OZRAF

BOOKS2READ

Connecting independent readers to independent writers.

Did you love *Living For God The Call To Be A Living Sacrifice*? Then you should read *A Christmas Journey of Faith*[1] by Joshua Rhoades!

In "A Christmas Journey of Faith", join four friends—Jake, Emma, Max, and Maya—on a thrilling time-travel adventure. When they discover a mysterious time machine hidden in an old shed, they embark on an incredible journey that takes them over 2,000 years into the past to witness the most important event in history: the birth of Jesus Christ. But this journey isn't just about seeing the past—it's about learning timeless lessons of faith, trust, and courage.

As they travel back to the time of Mary and Joseph, the friends witness the Christmas story unfold. From the angel Gabriel's visit to Mary to the long journey to Bethlehem and the miraculous birth of Jesus in a humble stable, they find themselves in the heart of the greatest

---

1. https://books2read.com/u/bWA9Qz

2. https://books2read.com/u/bWA9Qz

miracle. They stand in awe as the shepherds receive the good news from the angels, follow the star with the wise men, and learn how Mary and Joseph trusted God's plan, even when it was difficult.

Each step of their journey shows how faith in God can guide us through life's challenges. The friends learn that Christmas isn't about presents or decorations, but about the gift of Jesus, who came to bring peace, love, and hope to the world. As they experience these incredible events, they realize that God's love and salvation are for everyone—rich or poor, young or old.

"A Christmas Journey of Faith" is a heartwarming story that reminds readers of all ages to trust God's plan and embrace the true meaning of Christmas. Through the eyes of Jake, Emma, Max, and Maya, readers will be inspired to live out the message of salvation and faith that Jesus brought to the world.